Mao Zedong was the powerful leader of China from 1949 until his death in 1976. His image appeared everywhere, in every classroom, in every house, on every street.

COVER STORY

WHERE'S MAO?

But recently, when a reporter visited a classroom in Shanghai, he had one big question.

The reporter noticed that Mao was mentioned just briefly in the students' history books.

So what happened?

China had totally changed.

CHINA'S SECOND REVOLUTION

For one thing, the economy is booming. Under Mao, it was illegal to own a business. Now, it's encouraged. These days, students are more likely to learn about Bill Gates, chairman of Microsoft, than Chairman Mao.

How did this change come about? To find out, take a look back at some of the big milestones in China since the death of Mao. . . .

Book design: Red Herring Design/NYC

Library of Congress Cataloging-in-Publication Data
Population 1.3 billion : China becomes a super superpower.
p. om.   (24/7: behind the headlines: special edition)
Includes bibliographical references and index.
ISBN-13: 978-0-531-21806-8 (lib. bdg) 978-0-531-22002-3 (pbk.)
ISBN-10: 0-531-21806-6 (lib. bdg) 0-531-22002-8 (pbk.)
1. China—History—1976-2002—Juvenile literature.
2. China—History—2002—Juvenile literature. I. Title: Population one point
three billion. II. Title: China becomes a super superpower.
DS779.2.P67 2009
951.05—dc22
2008029027

POPULATION 1.3 BILLION

China Becomes a Super Superpower

Franklin Watts ®
An Imprint of Scholastic Inc.

CONTENTS

THE HEADLINES

In fewer than 30 years, China has become a modern superpower. How?

10 1976–1995: GOOD-BYE TO CHAIRMAN MAO

Chairman Mao dies . . . A new leader promises big changes . . . The government cracks down on a huge student-led protest . . .

26 1996–1999: TO GET RICH IS GLORIOUS

The standard of living is rising rapidly . . . Shanghai experiences a rebirth . . . Millions of people move from the country to the cities . . . A hero of the human rights movement is jailed . . .

THE 21ST CENTURY: THE CHINESE CENTURY?

38

Does everything in Wal-Mart really come from China? . . . The economic boom creates environmental problems . . . Beijing Olympics wow the world . . .

CHINA: FAQs

WHERE IS CHINA?

It is in eastern Asia. China, the world's fourth largest country, borders 14 different countries. Only one other nation—Russia—has that many neighbors.

HOW OLD IS CHINA?

Its civilization dates back at least 4,000 years. From the 3rd century B.C. until the early 1900s, a series of powerful emperors ruled China.

HOW BIG IS IT?

China is about the size of the United States, but has about four times as many people. With more than 1.3 billion citizens, it has the world's biggest population. One of every five people on Earth is Chinese.

WHAT KIND OF GOVERNMENT DOES IT HAVE?

The Chinese Communist Party (CCP) has been in power since 1949. It's a strict government that maintains tight control over political life. Many people outside the country criticize the government, saying that it denies people freedom of speech and other basic human rights.

CAN THE CHINESE PEOPLE VOTE?

Yes, but only at a local level. Citizens have no voice in China's national policies, which are decided by a few high-ranking members of the CCP.

SO MANY PRODUCTS ARE MADE IN CHINA. WHY IS THAT?

For most of the time that the CCP has been in power, the Chinese have lived in extreme poverty. In the 1970s, China made changes to its economic system that allowed many new businesses to be created. As a result, China now churns out thousands of products that are sold all over the world.

WHAT ARE THE BIGGEST PROBLEMS IN CHINA TODAY?

Like other countries that have industrialized quickly, China has terrible pollution. And while China's recent economic growth has created jobs for millions of city dwellers, most people in the countryside are still very poor. China is also criticized for its human rights record and lack of democracy.

CHINA: FACTS & FIGURES

A VAST LAND

China is the fourth largest country in the world. With 1.3 billion citizens, it's the world's most populous nation.

THE CHINESE FLAG: The red background represents the revolution that put communists into power in 1949. The large star stands for the Communist Party. The smaller stars represent the Chinese people.

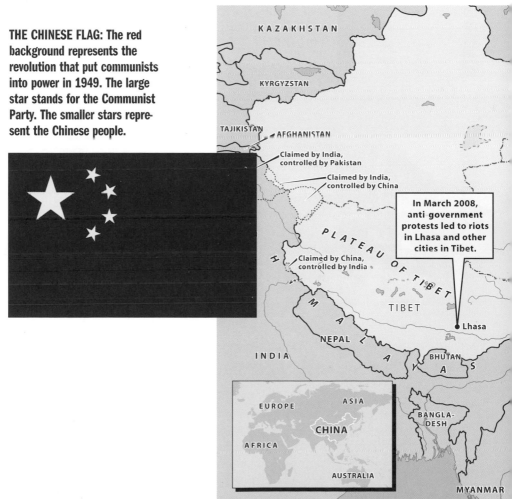

KAZAKHSTAN

KYRGYZSTAN

TAJIKISTAN · AFGHANISTAN

Claimed by India, controlled by Pakistan

Claimed by India, controlled by China

PLATEAU OF TIBET

In March 2008, anti government protests led to riots in Lhasa and other cities in Tibet.

Claimed by China, controlled by India

TIBET

Lhasa

H I M A L A Y A S

NEPAL

INDIA

BHUTAN

EUROPE

ASIA

CHINA

AFRICA

BANGLA-DESH

AUSTRALIA

MYANMAR

FACTS TO KNOW

OFFICIAL NAME: People's Republic of China

ETHNIC GROUPS: The Han Chinese make up 92% of the population. There are also 55 minority ethnic groups.

ECONOMY: China has the world's fourth largest gross national product (GNP). That's the value of all goods and services sold in a year.

LANGUAGES: 70% of the people speak Mandarin, the standard spoken Chinese. Other languages include Cantonese, Shanghainese, and Fujianese—all of which use the same written characters as Mandarin.

CITIES: There are more than 100 Chinese cities with populations of over 1,000,000. In the United States, there are just nine.

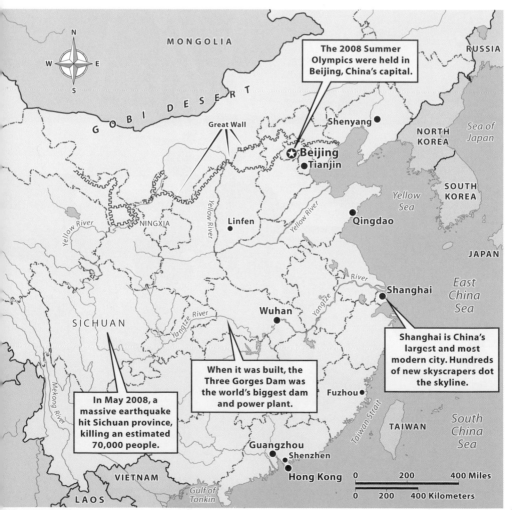

The 2008 Summer Olympics were held in Beijing, China's capital.

Shanghai is China's largest and most modern city. Hundreds of new skyscrapers dot the skyline.

When it was built, the Three Gorges Dam was the world's biggest dam and power plant.

In May 2008, a massive earthquake hit Sichuan province, killing an estimated 70,000 people.

GOOD-BYE TO CHAIRMAN MAO

THIS SECTION'S HEADLINE ARTICLES:

- ▸ Mao Dies
- ▸ Man of the Year
- ▸ Students Lead Massive Protest
- ▸ Crackdown!
- ▸ Under Close Watch
- ▸ The World's Youngest Political Prisoner

ON THE MARCH: In 1966, students known as Red Guards carried pictures of China's leader, Mao Zedong, through Beijing.

MAO DIES

How will his death change China?

RULE BY FORCE: Mao, seen here, once said, "Political power grows out of the barrel of a gun."

At 3 P.M. on September 18, 1976, China went silent. In factories and farms across the country, people were ordered to stop working. A million people stood quietly in Beijing's Tiananmen Square.

Then the sirens began wailing. For the next three minutes, ships, trains, and factories across the country sounded their whistles and horns. It was a tribute to China's leader, Mao Zedong, who died on September 9.

In his obituary, the government claimed that Mao's ideas would "forever illuminate the road [ahead] for the Chinese people."

But Mao's critics say that China suffered terrible hardships under his leadership and that his ideas should not shape its future.

A GREAT LEAP

When Mao was born in 1893, China was ruled by an emperor, just as it had been since the beginning of the 3rd century B.C.

In 1911, when Mao was 18, the emperor was overthrown. The country slipped into chaos. Many groups struggled for power. Foreign countries took over parts of China. The economy weakened, and there was more of a gap than ever between a few people who were very rich and the majority who were very poor.

In the early 1920s, Mao joined the Chinese Communist Party (CCP), which advocated a radical solution to China's problems—communism. Under that political system, all the land, houses, factories, and businesses belong to the government. All people are said to be equal, and the government is supposed to provide everyone with a job, a home, and food.

In 1949, after China had experienced decades of war and hardship, the CCP came to power, backed by millions of poor farmers.

Now the leader of the CCP, Mao set out to turn China into a modern industrialized nation, based on communist ideas. And between 1953 and 1957, the country made real progress. In the cities, the government took over privately owned factories—and industry thrived.

But in the countryside, there was disaster. Peasants were moved onto large farms called collectives. These farms were badly run, and no good system for distributing food existed. Thirty million people starved to death.

By 1966, Mao faced fierce critics. He used a movement called the Cultural Revolution to strengthen his position. He recruited young people, called Red Guards, to identify critics of the government—even their own parents and teachers. Schools were closed, and economic production slowed. Hundreds of thousands of people were humiliated, tortured, and killed.

Now, in 1976, many Chinese people joke that Mao did make them all equal—equally poor, that is. They long for stability and prosperity and are ready for a leader who will take China in a new direction.

13

MAN OF THE YEAR

Deng Xiaoping

leads China in a new direction.

NEW LEADER: Deng Xiaoping
reviews troops in 1984.

Time magazine has named Deng Xiaoping, China's leader, as 1985's Man of the Year.

Deng has been on *Time*'s cover several times before. Yet few people in the West know much about him. Unlike Chairman Mao, Deng doesn't draw attention to himself. He prefers for people to focus on the changes he has brought about since Mao's death.

After Deng became China's leader in 1978, he set about trying to repair China's broken economy. He wanted to modernize the country and lift its people out of poverty. Because of his policies, people who used to fantasize about owning a watch or a radio can now afford refrigerators and TV sets.

A BROKEN ECONOMY

For many years, Deng was a loyal party leader under Mao, but the

OLD WAYS: Under Mao, farmers were forced to work on group farms, as shown in this 1965 photo.

two men did not always agree about economic issues.

Under Mao, the Communist Party had total control of the economy. People weren't allowed to run their own businesses or to make a profit. Farmers and factory bosses couldn't make their own decisions.

Mao's goal was to fix China's longtime economic problems, and at first some of his policies were successful. But many of them eventually failed, leading to widespread suffering and starvation.

Deng saw that the market-driven, capitalist economies of Western countries worked better. In these economies, individuals or companies own and run businesses—and they're motivated to improve their businesses in order to make more money. Also, busi-

nesses in these economies compete with each other. That motivates them to provide the best products and services.

Deng urged Mao to introduce some capitalist policies into the Chinese economy. "It does not matter whether the cat is black or white," Deng said, "so long as it catches mice." In other words, it didn't matter whether the economy was communist or capitalist—just as long as it helped people make a living.

Some of Deng's reforms were enacted, but in 1967 Mao denounced Deng for "taking the capitalist road," and Deng was sent away to work at a factory.

"TO GET RICH IS GLORIOUS"

It wasn't until Deng became China's leader in 1978 that he was

15

able to continue on that road. "To get rich is glorious!" he proclaimed. He announced sweeping changes. Today, the group farms are gone and farmers are free to profit from their crops. As a result, their incomes have tripled. The government has given greater responsibility to local factory managers, and industry is growing rapidly. Many people own their own businesses.

But Deng's most radical change has been to open China to the outside world. Trade is encouraged. Foreign companies are building factories in China and investing in its industries. Tourists are welcome.

Most Chinese are still poor, but Deng's reforms are helping many people to fulfill their

REFRESHING: Coca-Cola is one of many U.S. products now on sale in China.

dreams. Yip Hongcheung, from Guangdong province, is a good example. She points with pride to her two-story home, new stereo, and indoor plumbing. "Before I could only dream of such things," she says.

NEW THINGS: A rural couple carries home a prize possession— their first TV.

STUDENTS LEAD
MASSIVE
PROTEST

A MILLION STRONG: Led by college students, a huge crowd gathers in Beijing's Tiananmen Square to demand government reforms.

Protest enters its seventh week.

It's late May 1989, and the eyes of the world are on Beijing's Tiananmen Square. Hundreds of thousands of Chinese students and workers are gathered there for a massive pro-democracy demonstration. Many people have been camped out in the square for six weeks.

They have braved heat, hunger, and other hardships to make their voices heard.

China's leaders are furious about being criticized in front of the whole world. And they are losing patience. The government has moved 300,000 soldiers into the city.

A BETTER FUTURE: Student protesters want their government to fight corruption and speed up its democratic reforms.

The question now is—will Deng Xiaoping use force to crush the protest? Or will he agree to make the reforms that the students are demanding?

THE PROTESTS SPREAD

The uprising began in mid-April, shortly after the death of Hu Yaobang. He was a Communist Party official who was fired by Deng for siding with student protesters in 1985 and 1986.

On April 17, students at Beijing University held a memorial service for Hu. During the gathering, some participants forcefully criticized the government. The service became a protest, attracting thousands. Eventually, the huge crowd relocated to Tiananmen Square.

The flames of protest spread quickly, sparking demonstrations in 36 other cities. Soon the total number of protesters had swelled to a million people.

LIFE IN THE SQUARE

The atmosphere in the square is festive. There are acrobats and rock bands. Children bang on drums. Students make speeches and chant slogans. Some wave banners that declare, "Give me democracy or give me death!"

One participant, 23-year-old Chai Ling, described the scene

this way: "You could see many people together, parents holding their babies, friends holding hands. You felt so safe. There was no fear, no danger. You felt connected to everybody."

Despite the carnival atmosphere, the protesters are serious about their goals. Many are on hunger strikes. They hope their refusal to eat will force the government to listen to them.

WHAT DO THEY WANT?

A government-run newspaper called the movement "a rebellion aimed at destroying communism." But the protesters say they want to reform the government, not bring it down.

They accuse government officials of being corrupt. They say that many leaders use their positions to make themselves rich, and that they give all the best jobs to their friends and families.

The protesters are also demanding more rights. They want a more democratic government, with leaders elected by the people. They also want the freedom to criticize these leaders.

With the media focused on the protesters—and people around the world cheering them on—Deng

has to be careful. A violent crackdown by the army could turn public opinion against China.

But student leaders fear that troops will soon march into Tiananmen Square. They are talking about calling off the demonstration before it's too late.

HIGH HOPES: Protesters built a 33-foot tall statue—the "Goddess of Democracy"—as a symbol of their hopes for freedom.

19

SHEER COURAGE: In June 1989, the world watched as a single protester stood in the way of tanks entering Tiananmen Square.

CRACKDOWN!

China's government crushes student-led democracy movement.

On June 3, 1989, at about 10:30 P.M., Chinese troops and tanks moved through the capital city of Beijing, headed for Tiananmen Square.

The tanks smashed through barricades protesters had constructed to block streets around the square. Soldiers shot tear gas and bullets into crowds of civilian demonstrators.

"From where I was, the sound of crying was louder than the gunfire," said one witness. "I kept seeing people falling. What I saw was bodies, bodies, bodies."

Some of the injured were saved by rickshaw drivers. Rickshaws are bicycle carts used to transport passengers, and these drivers risked their lives to step into the line of fire and take the wounded to hospitals.

By early in the morning of June 4, the soldiers had cleared Tiananmen Square.

THE OFFICIAL STORY

Chinese officials have presented their own version of the night. They say that the protest leaders

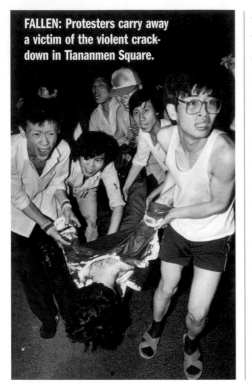

FALLEN: Protesters carry away a victim of the violent crackdown in Tiananmen Square.

were "rioters" and "hooligans." They also claim that the soldiers were only defending themselves from attacks by students—and never "fired directly at the people."

The government also denied that many people were killed. It is impossible to know the exact number of fatalities. However, one estimate puts the figure at 1,000.

In the days following the crackdown, the police arrested tens of thousands of protesters.

U.S. President George H. W. Bush joined other world leaders in condemning China's actions. But for now, the democracy movement has been crushed.

"The Bullets Are Real"
An eyewitness in Beijing remembers.

Shen Tong was a student leader of the uprising. In his book, *Almost a Revolution*, he describes the crackdown. He tells how tanks bore down on the protesters, as the students hurried to put up barricades.

Then the machine-gun fire began—and the protesters scattered. Shen looked on in disbelief as people who had been shot stumbled to the ground and lay motionless. *Those people are dead,* he thought. *The bullets are real.* It all seemed like a terrible dream.

STUDENT LEADER: Shen Tong describes the crackdown in a book he wrote about the protest.

21

UNDER CLOSE WATCH

The Chinese still lack many basic rights.

LOOMING PRESENCE: Huge murals of leader Deng Xiaoping remind people of the government's control over their lives.

Three years after the crackdown in Tiananmen Square, the Chinese government is still punishing people who challenge its authority. That's what Asia Watch's 1992 report says. Asia Watch is a group that monitors how governments treat their people.

In the past 15 years, China's growing economy has dramatically improved life for most people. Millions have new jobs and better opportunities.

But one thing hasn't changed—China's policy on human rights. These are basic freedoms that most Americans take for granted: the right to speak your mind, to practice your religion, and to be given a fair trial if you're accused of a crime. China's government generally denies people those rights. Just talking with a foreigner about human rights can land a person in jail.

The Asia Watch report was written by Tang Boqiao, a leader of the Chinese democracy movement who spent a year in jail for his political activities. He says that thousands of dissidents—critics of the government—have been imprisoned since the crackdown.

BEHIND BARS

Tang reports that torture is sometimes used to get dissidents to confess to anti-government activities—and that they are often put in jail without benefit of a trial.

In jail, Tang saw some prisoners being beaten. He also often saw prisoners chained to steel bars. "Some were shackled this way for as long as a month," he writes in his report.

Many members of the U.S. Congress are horrified by the abuses reported by Asia Watch. They want the U.S. to stop trading with China until it improves its human rights record. But President George H. W. Bush opposes a ban on trade. He believes that the best way to encourage political reform in China is to support its economic growth.

Stock Market Soaring
New investors snap up stocks.

May 1993—The Shanghai Stock Exchange is booming. In the first three months of this year, more than twice as many stocks were traded than in all of 1992.

Two million Chinese have invested in the market since it opened in 1990. Millions more are hoping to get a piece of the action. "In time, it's going to be Asia's biggest stock market," one businessman told the *New York Times*.

Most shareholders have invested small amounts. But some high rollers are becoming rich. "Today I made [$20,000]," Yang Huaiding, a former member of Mao's Red Guards, told the *Times*. "Not bad for a day!"

BUYING IN: This board at the Shanghai Stock Exchange lists prices for shares of stock in Chinese companies.

GEDHUN CHOEKYI NYIMA:
Tibetan leaders decided he
was the Panchen Lama.

THE WORLD'S YOUNGEST POLITICAL PRISONER
Young Tibetan leader is seized.

In June 1995, Chinese security forces swept into Tibet and took away a six-year-old boy and his family. The child hasn't been seen since. Human rights groups say China is holding him under house arrest.

What does China have to fear from a little boy? Well, Gedhun Choekyi Nyima is no ordinary kid. To many, he represents Tibet's opposition to Chinese control.

Since 1911, Tibet had been mostly free of Chinese control. But in 1950, under Mao's leadership, China invaded and took over this region, which is roughly the size of Washington, Oregon, California, and Arizona combined. Chinese leaders forced the religious and political leader—a Tibetan Buddhist called the Dalai Lama—to accept Chinese rule in Tibet.

Still, most Tibetans stayed loyal to the Dalai Lama. Even after the Dalai Lama fled to India in 1959, Tibetans considered him their leader. They also remained loyal to the Panchen Lama, the second-most important leader in Tibetan Buddhism.

In 1989, the Panchen Lama died. According to Tibetan

GYALTSEN NORBU: Chinese officials picked *him* to be the Panchen Lama.

Buddhists, when an important leader like a Panchen Lama dies, his spirit is reincarnated—transferred to another person, usually a baby. So religious leaders looked for Tibetan boys born around the time of his death. They found Gedhun Choekyi Nyima and decided he was the new Panchen Lama.

Chinese leaders panicked. They didn't want Tibetans to develop loyalty to another Tibetan leader they couldn't control. So they took Gedhun Choekyi Nyima prisoner. Then they held a ceremony to introduce six-year-old Gyaltsen Norbu, whom they said was the new incarnation of the Panchen Lama. Their plan is to raise him to be loyal to the Chinese government.

Chinese officials say Gedhun Choekyi Nyima is alive and well but have offered no evidence. "I am really concerned about the poor boy's safety," the Dalai Lama told the *New York Times*.

LEADER IN EXILE: Tenzin Gyatso, the Dalai Lama, greets followers in India.

TO GET RICH IS GLORIOUS

THIS SECTION'S HEADLINE ARTICLES:

- ▸ Living the Chinese Dream
- ▸ Flocking to the Cities
- ▸ Building the World's Biggest Dam
- ▸ Imprisoned!
- ▸ Can the Internet Free China?

A NEW LOOK: Models walk the runway in a 1996 fashion show in Beijing. In the 1990s, a booming economy brought luxury items to members of China's elite.

LIVING THE CHINESE DREAM

China's fast-growing economy is lifting millions out of poverty.

ON THE TOWN: A young couple enjoys the nightlife in Shenzhen. The city is home to many of the businesses that have fueled China's economic boom.

Unlike his parents, Geng Mengfei, 12, has never experienced poverty. "My parents spend lots of money on me," Mengfei says.

For his birthday, Mengfei's parents gave him a piano worth more than $1,200. Of course even now, in 1996, that type of luxury is still too expensive for most Chinese. But since the reforms of the 1980s, China's economy—now the fastest growing in the world— has lifted millions out of poverty.

Mengfei's mother remembers life before the reforms. "[It] was very hard," she says. "The central government issued coupons to city people. Every month, each person in Beijing got coupons to buy wheat, corn, a small bottle of cooking oil, and some cloth [to make clothes]."

Since 1949, China has had a communist government. And for almost 30 years, the government controlled all businesses and jobs. Citizens were not allowed to own or work for private businesses. Workers could earn only as much

NICE WHEELS! At a 1996 car show, people admire one of the first sports cars to be built in China.

money as the government would pay. Often, that was barely enough to survive.

Much has changed since then. Today, the government encourages people to work for themselves and make as much money as they can.

Mengfei's family is a good example. A few years ago, Mengfei's father took a big risk. He quit his safe government job and borrowed money from relatives. He bought sweaters and jackets in southern China, where they were made.

ON THE LINE: Workers assemble dolls that will be sold around the world.

Flocking to the Cities
China's cities are exploding with people from the countryside.

In the Chinese countryside, money is so scarce that one false move can mean disaster. "Our cow fell off a cliff, and we can't plow the land now," says Chen Cuilan, 11.

So Cuilan's mother left home to get a job in the city. She is not alone. Since the economic reforms began, many factories have been built in the cities along China's eastern coastline. More than 100 million peasants have moved to these cities to find jobs and escape rural poverty.

As cities grow, so does the economy. Migrants provide cheap labor for expanding businesses. They also buy lots of goods and services.

The great migration has its downside. China's cities are over-crowded. Crime rates and pollution are on the rise. Still, for millions of Chinese, the city is the only place to be.

Then he sold them in Beijing. Soon, his company was thriving.

Newly arrived foreign businesses have also boosted China's prosperity. Mengfei's neighborhood in Beijing now has lots of new shops and restaurants. He can grab fast food at the local Kentucky Fried Chicken or McDonald's. And he owns many things his parents could never have afforded when they were his age. "I can buy lots of stuff," he says.

NATIONAL PRIDE

Hao Yun is an elementary school student in Beijing. Like Mengfei, she has seen her family's standard of living improve a lot. Her parents, who are accountants, have been able to buy a car—a real luxury in today's China. And the family has moved to a much bigger apartment.

Another big change in Yun's life has been access to foreign TV shows. Television and movies have given young people a window on the outside world that previously did not exist. Yun's favorite show is *Baywatch*.

Yun takes a photography class in school and likes to take photos "that show the changes in our country, like the new high-rise buildings." Like millions of other Chinese people, she is very proud of those changes.

LOVIN' IT: Chinese teens enjoy fast food at a McDonald's in Shanghai.

BUILDING THE WORLD'S BIGGEST DAM
Plant will provide electricity for millions.

Last year, in 1995, China began construction on the Three Gorges Dam. Located on the Yangtze—Asia's longest river—it will be the world's biggest dam as well as its biggest power plant.

The dam is being built where the Yangtze rushes through a series of steep gorges. It will be more than a mile (1.6 km) wide and will create a huge lake almost 400 miles (645 km) long. As the lake fills up, it will flood hundreds of villages and towns. About 1.3 million people will have to abandon their homes. That would be like telling every person in the state of New Hampshire to move.

Supporters of the dam say that China's economic boom depends on having plenty of electricity. They estimate that the dam's power plant will supply up to ten percent of the power China needs.

But the dam also has many critics. They argue that in addition to displacing people, the immense project will seriously damage the environment. And they say that the power plant will supply only about three percent of China's electricity.

RISING WATERS: The Three Gorges Dam will supply as much electricity as 15 coal-burning power stations.

1997: Three Lives

The lives of these three people reflect the new China.

Liu Yongxing: A New Businessman

In 1982, Liu Yongxing and his brothers decided to act on Deng's slogan, "To get rich is glorious!" So they sold their watches and bicycles for $120, bought a few quail, and hatched a bird-raising business.

Today, that once-tiny operation is the Hope Group, China's largest private company. It produces animal feed and employs 10,000 workers. Liu and his brothers are millionaires. "When I sold my bicycle and watch, I never thought I would end up like this," Liu says. "I just wanted to raise quail."

Chen Xi: Privilege and Pressure

Chen Xi, 18, loves to show off his new Nike Air Max running shoes—along with his TV, VCR, stereo, and computer. His generation is the first to enjoy such possessions. When Chen's parents were growing up, many people didn't even have shoes.

But Chen has limited time to enjoy his stuff. He's under a lot of pressure to get ahead. He's been studying for a super-competitive national university entrance exam. "If you fail," Chen says, "you spend another year preparing to take the test again."

Dai Qing: Government Critic

Dai Qing, 56, began her career as a reporter for a Communist Party newspaper. But instead of writing what the government told her to, she uncovered stories of corruption and human-rights abuses.

In 1989, Dai wrote a book about the environmental dangers of the proposed Three Gorges Dam project. Not long after, she was thrown in jail for a year. She says her book was the reason.

Government officials have banned Dai's writing in China. But Dai promises to keep working. "The [government] tries to cover things up," she says, "and [my job] is to try to dig them up."

IMPRISONED!

AWAITING A VERDICT: Xu Wenli posed for this photo just weeks before being sent back to jail.

Human rights activist is sent to prison—again.

Xu Wenli, a hero of the human rights movement in China, was sentenced to 13 years in prison today, December 21, 1998.

He was found guilty of helping to organize a pro-democracy political party and of pushing for an end to communist rule. It's not the first time Xu has been imprisoned for his beliefs.

Xu grew up loyal to the Chinese Communist Party. But everything changed on April 5, 1976, when he saw police brutally beating anti-government protesters in Beijing. "At that moment, I realized that everything I believed was a lie," Xu has said.

In 1978, Xu and other activists

launched the "Democracy Wall" movement. With the approval of Deng Xiaoping, they glued posters and essays calling for change on the wall of a compound where many Chinese leaders lived. Xu also began publishing a pro-democracy newspaper.

In 1981, Xu was arrested and sentenced to 15 years in prison.

In jail, Xu endured solitary confinement and harsh interrogations. He was released three years early—in 1993—and told to leave the country. Xu refused. Instead, he started an organization to monitor human rights in China. It used fax machines and computers to connect activists throughout the country.

Then in June 1998, Xu helped form the China Democracy Party, which he described as "a mature, steady, responsible, constructive, legal opposition [party]." He was arrested a short time later.

"I Couldn't Keep from Crying"
Xu Wenli's daughter wants her father freed.

DEC 1998—Xu Jin, Xu Wenli's daughter, has lived in the United States since she left China in 1994. She's been speaking out for her father, pressuring China to free him. Xu Jin told the *New York Times* that the first time her father was in jail, she and her mother were allowed to see him for only 40 minutes every two months. She recalled one visit in 1989: "I couldn't keep myself from crying," she said. "His hair was gray, a lot of his teeth had fallen out, and his hand was shaking."

SPEAKING OUT: Xu Jin and another human rights activist speak to the press, demanding that China release her father. (Xu Wenli was finally freed in 2002. He joined his family in the U.S. and continues to push for democracy in China.)

CAN THE INTERNET FREE CHINA?

The government struggles to control access to information.

The Chinese government has long kept an iron grip on the country's media. But as China celebrates 50 years of communist rule, government censors are facing a major challenge: the Internet.

By strictly controlling all books, newspapers, TV shows, and radio broadcasts, China's leaders have tried to prevent citizens from speaking out against the government. But now, millions of Chinese have Internet access—and some are using websites and email to share information and to discuss democracy and free speech. "The impact is revolutionary," says one human rights activist. "The Internet has created a public space for discussion, which China has never had."

THE GREAT FIREWALL

Chinese officials have responded by forming special security units to fight the spread of anti-government information. They have built an electronic "firewall" to stop Internet users from visiting websites that the government dislikes. They have even jailed citizens for using the Internet to criticize the government. But many computer users know how to get past the firewall. And email is very hard to control.

Why doesn't China just ban the Internet? Technology is too important in the business world. Banning the Internet would badly damage China's economy.

Experts predict that more than 200 million people in China will be online within a few years. What will that mean? There will be much more "independent thinking" in China, says Xiao Qiang, a pro-democracy activist.

Shanghai Express
China's largest city gets a makeover.

24/7: Unlike most airports, Pudong International is open around the clock.

OCT 1999—After just two years of construction, Shanghai's second international airport is open for business. Eventually, it will be able to handle 80 million passengers a year.

In 1992, China's leader, Deng Xiaoping, said Shanghai should "take faster steps" toward modernization. Since then, the residents of this major seaport have lived with the clamor of constant construction as thousands of workers—and half the world's high-rise cranes—built a new skyline.

Most of the city's new office towers, hotels, and subways are being built in the Pudong district, which was an open countryside just a decade ago. Today, the area is a cross between "Disneyland and New York City," according to one MSNBC reporter.

THE CHINESE CENTURY?

THIS SECTION'S HEADLINE ARTICLES:

- ▸ Getting Ahead
- ▸ A New Day for Girls
- ▸ The Diary of Ma Yan
- ▸ Choking on Progress
- ▸ Smackdown!
- ▸ China Wows the World

SUPERPOWER SKYLINE: With its glittering skyscrapers, Shanghai is a symbol of the country's emergence as a global economic power. Shanghai is China's biggest city and the world's biggest port.

GETTING AHEAD

Chinese students feel the pressure to succeed.

In Mao's China, the government guaranteed people jobs for life. That's no longer the case. Students know they will face an extremely competitive job market when they graduate.

The fast-growing economy has created millions of new jobs. But there are many qualified applicants for each job. So students are under intense pressure to excel in school.

AN UPHILL BATTLE

Liu Li, 15, lives with her family in the countryside. Her parents are farmers, and like many rural

BIG DREAMS: Liu Li lives on a farm in southwestern China. She wants to be a doctor.

BOOKED UP: Li Wenliang goes to one of the best schools in Beijing. He has 12 hours of classes every day.

Chinese, they are poor.

Li hopes to become a doctor. That means that school is her life. Except on weekends and holidays, she spends nine hours in class every day.

She's a good student, but fulfilling her ambition will be difficult. Li's rural school is so poor that it doesn't have computers—or heat! Money is tight at home, too. Li has never even visited the nearby city of Chengdu, just a short bus ride away.

FIERCE COMPETITION

Li Wenliang, 11, lives in Beijing. His father is a lawyer, and his mother is a scientist. They are wealthy even by city standards.

Like Liu Li, Wenliang hopes to become a doctor. But his chances are better than Li's. Wenliang goes to one of the best public schools in Beijing. His school has computers, a swimming pool, and enough money to send students on field trips.

Still, competition to get into universities is fierce. Only about one in four students who take the entrance exams gets in. So even a privileged city kid has to study hard. Wenliang has classes from 8 A.M. to 8 P.M. every weekday.

"The pressure on our generation is greater than it was on our parents, since you can't depend on the government anymore," says Chu Chen Deng, 19. "With the new economy, if you have no culture and no skills, it's hard to earn a living."

AMBITIOUS: Chu Chen Deng is learning the job skills he'll need to succeed in China's competitive economy.

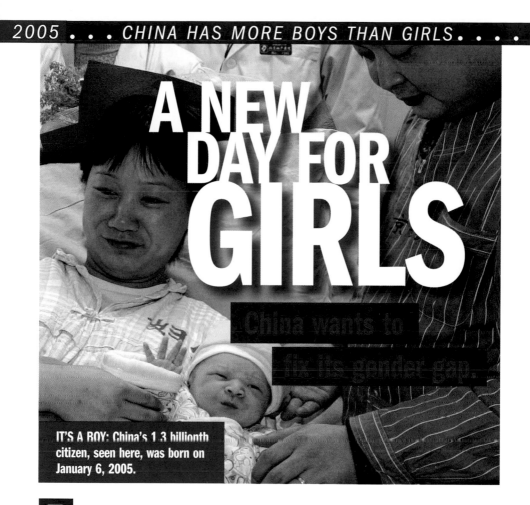

A NEW DAY FOR GIRLS

China wants to fix its gender gap.

IT'S A BOY: China's 1.3 billionth citizen, seen here, was born on January 6, 2005.

In 2005, China celebrated the birth of its 1.3 billionth citizen. The baby was a boy. That was no surprise. In China, 119 boys are born for every 100 girls. (The worldwide average is 105 boys per 100 girls.) In just a few decades, the nation could have 40 million bachelors who cannot find wives.

Experts blame China's gender imbalance on the government's "one-child policy," which limits most couples to one child. (The policy was enacted to control the country's population.) Many Chinese parents prefer sons. In rural areas, families want sons to do farmwork. And elderly parents throughout the country rely on sons to take care of them. In China, daughters traditionally help care for their husbands' parents. Sons care for their own.

For some Chinese parents, having only one child means mak-

ing sure it's a boy. Some parents put baby girls up for adoption. Others choose abortion if they know they are having a girl.

CLOSING THE GAP

For years, the government ignored the widening gender gap. But in March 2005, it formed a research group to study the problem.

The group may look at whether China should shift to a two-child policy for all families. In rural areas, most families are already allowed to have a second child if their first is a girl. The government is also testing a program that gives yearly payments to elderly rural people who have no sons.

"It used to be that if you had girls, you were looked down upon," says one official. But new policies are changing that attitude—and many parents are learning to value girls as much as boys.

RETURN TO CHINA
Anna was adopted from China as a baby. Twelve years later, she went back.

Anna DeSanctis has lived in Houston with her adoptive parents since she was a baby. But Anna began her life in China.

Like so many Chinese girls, Anna was left in an orphanage soon after she was born. She doesn't know why her birth parents gave her up. "Was it just because I was a girl?" she wonders. But she doesn't dwell on it. What matters is that she loves her current life.

In 2003, Anna began raising money to help orphans in China. Three years later, she traveled there and opened new libraries in four orphanages.

"I will never forget the faces of children seeing books for the first time," she says.

GIVING BACK: One of the libraries that Anna DeSanctis helped build is in the city where she was born.

THE DIARY OF MA YAN

A young writer finds success.

DEAR DIARY: The diary of Ma Yan (in pink jacket) has been published in 17 languages.

Ma Yan is a young writer from a village in Ningxia, a rural province. When she began keeping a diary at age 12, her parents were too poor to buy her a pen. So Ma Yan skipped lunch for two weeks and used her lunch money to buy one.

China's economy is booming. But about 300 million Chinese people still live in poverty. Most poor Chinese, like Ma Yan's family, live in the country. Average rural incomes are only one-third the size of typical city incomes. Many rural people are too poor to afford heat and running water. Some have never been to a doctor.

HER WAY OUT

Ma Yan began writing her diary in 2000, when she was a student at a boarding school. All students were required to keep journals.

Ma Yan's parents were struggling farm workers. They could barely afford her tuition. Ma Yan had only one outfit to wear in school. Some days, she and her brother had no money for lunch. "The comrades are all eating, and we have to stand by and grit our teeth," she wrote. "Do you know what hunger is? It's an unbearable pain."

Despite the hardships, Ma Yan was thrilled to be in school. She knew that an education was her only way out of grinding poverty.

But Ma Yan's parents eventually ran out of money, and she had to leave school. She was very upset.

ON TOUR: Ma Yan attends a book fair in Paris in 2004.

A STROKE OF LUCK

In 2001, a journalist visiting Ningxia read Ma Yan's diary. He was so moved by her story that he offered to pay her tuition. He also arranged for the diary to be published in France. And this year, 2005, *The Diary of Ma Yan: The Struggles and Hopes of a Chinese Schoolgirl* has been published in the United States.

Because of Ma Yan's success, her family is no longer poor. "I can eat when I want to. My parents have bought some land," she says. Ma Yan is also helping 250 teens from her province pay for school.

45

PIECE WORK: A young worker assembles shoes at a factory in Guangdong province.

THE WORLD'S WORKSHOP

The "Made in China" label is everywhere. How did that happen?

Do you ever shop at Wal-Mart? If so, you're part of the booming Chinese economy. More than 70 percent of the products that line the shelves of the giant chain are made in China, according to a November 2004 report in *China Business Daily*.

And it's not just Wal-Mart. Go into any store and try to find a cell phone, a toaster, or a toy *not* made in China. It isn't easy.

WHY CHINA?

Why are so many goods sold in the U.S. made in China? It's because of what some people call the "China price." That's the amount that Chinese companies charge to make a product. And these days, it's often much cheaper to make a product in China than in the United States.

As a result, U.S. companies like Wal-Mart, Reebok, and others are stampeding to China to set

up factories there. Today, China assembles more toys, stitches more shoes, and sews more clothes than any other nation—all for the low, low China price.

China doesn't only make products for foreign companies. It also has its own industries that sell products at home and abroad. Wanfeng, a Chinese car company, makes an SUV that sells for $9,000. Compare it with the very similar U.S.-made Chrysler Jeep Grand Cherokee. Price tag: $32,000.

How can Chinese manufacturers make so many products—and so cheaply? For starters, there's China's huge population: 1.3 billion. That's an almost endless supply of laborers. And compared with workers in the United States, they earn very low salaries. In the U.S., labor laws and labor unions guarantee workers higher wages. That can drive up the cost of American-made goods.

What's more, the cost of fuel, steel, and other materials is lower in China.

Will China's extraordinary boom continue? Most experts say yes. In 20 years, many predict, China will overtake the U.S. to become the world's largest economy.

China Makes; You Take

Not everything for sale in U.S. stores is made in China. It just seems that way!

TOY FACTORY: Most of the world's dolls are made in China.

Thousands of products are made in Chinese factories. Look at how many popular items come from China:

83% of the world's laptops

70% of the world's buttons

40% of the apple juice in U.S. stores

80% of the toys in U.S. stores

90% of the vitamin C in U.S. stores

72% of the shoes in U.S. stores

CHOKING ON PROGRESS

China struggles to control its pollution.

TOXIC SMOG: Cyclists in Jiangsu province wear masks to protect their lungs. Like other countries that have industrialized quickly, China has terrible pollution.

RIVER OF FILTH: Fishermen sit by a waterway clogged with garbage.

In the past, industrial countries have learned a hard lesson: manufacturing can lead to terrible pollution. In Ohio, for example, the Cuyahoga River actually caught fire several times in the 20th century because it was so polluted with industrial waste.

China's rapid industrialization has also come at a high price. Thick smog from cars and factories blankets most cities. Bicyclists wear masks to protect their lungs. By Western standards, only one percent of China's city dwellers have clean air to breathe.

The water is just as dirty. Almost 500 million Chinese people are living—and dying—without safe drinking water. About 70 percent of China's rivers and lakes are polluted. In large areas along the coast, all plant and animal life in the sea has died.

A GLOBAL ISSUE

China's pollution doesn't stay within the nation's borders. It's becoming a problem for the world. Acid rain, filled with chemicals from China's power plants, falls on the Korean Peninsula and Japan. Rivers carrying toxins from Chinese factories cross the border into Russia. On some days, almost 25 percent of the smog in Los Angeles can be traced to China!

By 2010, if not sooner, China will become the world's leading producer of greenhouse gases. These gases, which trap the sun's heat, are a major factor in global warming.

WHAT HAPPENS NEXT?

China needs to clean up its act—fast! Otherwise, one expert warns, pollution levels could quadruple in the next 15 years. The government is taking steps to close coal

49

mines (a major source of pollution) and to develop clean energy sources, such as wind and solar power. Fuel-efficiency standards for cars are already stricter than in the United States.

But going green is going to be tricky. Government leaders fear that passing strict environmental laws will hurt the economy and anger citizens.

Not that Chinese citizens aren't already angry about the poisons they breathe and drink. In 2005, people in a town in southern China protested plans to build a power plant nearby. Government security forces cracked down, killing 20 people. It was the deadliest use of force against Chinese citizens since the Tiananmen Square massacre in 1989. And the situation can only get uglier as China gets dirtier.

STUCK: Beijing commuters in a rush-hour traffic jam.

Crazy for Cars
More and more Chinese are buying cars.

Before the boom, most Chinese people used bicycles and public transit to get around. Private car ownership was illegal. Few could afford a car, anyway. Today, China's middle class has fallen in love with cars. That's good news for car companies, but bad news for the environment. Check out these facts about China and cars:

Number of privately owned cars in 1984: **virtually zero**

Number of privately owned cars in 2006: **11.5 million**

Expected number of privately owned cars in 2015: **150 million**

Percentage of urban air pollution caused by cars in 2004: **50**

SCREENING OUT: A view of Google's Chinese homepage in 2006.

SMACKDOWN!

U.S. Congress scolds Yahoo! and Google.

"Are you ashamed?" thundered Congressman Tom Lantos at a stormy hearing conducted by the U.S. House of Representatives in February 2006.

Lantos wasn't scolding a criminal or hounding a political opponent. He was shouting at an executive from Google, the world's most popular search engine.

Lantos was infuriated that Google is helping China to censor political content and restrict free speech on the Internet. Microsoft and Yahoo! were also summoned to the hearing to face the wrath of Congress.

Google's representatives said they censor only because Chinese law demands it. If they didn't follow the rules, China would shut them down—and Google claims that would leave Chinese citizens with even less access to information than they have now.

POLICING THE INTERNET

China operates the world's largest online censorship system. Taken together, the laws, surveillance,

51

and technology that limit online freedom in China are called the Great Firewall.

How does the Great Firewall work? China has an Internet police force of 30,000. These cops read personal emails, shut down websites that are critical of the government, and arrest people for using the Internet to speak out against the Chinese Communist Party.

American companies have helped build the Great Firewall. The Chinese version of Google's search engine filters out web pages that break government rules. Microsoft purged the terms *democracy* and *human rights* from its Chinese blog-hosting service. Yahoo! gave officials the email address of a Chinese journalist who was communicating with pro-democracy groups in the U.S.—and now the man is serving a ten-year prison term.

Despite the criticism from Congress, Google and the other companies continue to follow China's rules. But Chinese authorities may be unable to stop the free flow of information. There are 200 million Chinese Internet users, and more log on every day. Government censors could soon find themselves overwhelmed.

Cyber Snoops
Some students help government censors.

SEPT 2006—*Snitch*. That's what many people would call Hu Yingying

Hu is one of 500 students at Shanghai Normal University to volunteer as an Internet monitor. She polices her school's computer bulletin boards. When she finds something that insults China or breaks other rules, she turns the offender in to the authorities.

"We don't control things," she says, "but we don't want bad or wrong things on the Web."

CAUGHT YOU! Student spies keep an eye on their peers.

LEVELED: Rescuers search the wreckage for survivors.

CHINA'S AGONY

A massive earthquake devastates China.

At 2:28 P.M. on May 19, 2008, people all over China stopped what they were doing and stood in silence for three minutes. Many of them cried.

They were remembering the victims of the massive earthquake that rocked Sichuan province a week earlier, on May 12. Many buildings were flattened, and nearly 70,000 people were killed. An estimated five million people lost their homes.

Thousands of children were killed when their schools collapsed. In many cases, nearby buildings remained standing. Many parents charged that corrupt politicians had allowed schools to be built with cheap materials. "The concrete was like talcum powder, and the steel was as thin as noodles," said a parent who lost his son. At one memorial service, parents wore T-shirts that read: "Punish the corrupt people who put up this flimsy building."

Foreign observers praised the government's rescue efforts as well as its unusual openness about the tragedy. Scenes of the disaster and relief operations have been broadcast around the clock. As one British journalist noted, such coverage is "unprecedented in China."

GRIEVING: This woman's son was killed when his school collapsed.

CHINA WOWS THE WORLD

Two billion TV viewers watch spectacular Olympic ceremony.

BIG MOMENT: NBA star Yao Ming, an icon in his native China, carries its flag during the opening ceremonies. The boy with him, Lin Hao, survived the massive earthquake in May 2008.

IN UNISON: The spectacular opening ceremonies included 2,008 drummers.

For China, July 2001 was a time to celebrate. That's when the International Olympic Committee selected Beijing as the site of the 2008 Summer Olympics. Hosting the Olympics would be an historic first for China—and an opportunity to proclaim that this once-impoverished nation was now a major player on the world stage.

Over the next seven years, the Chinese government would spend more than 40 billion dollars building stadiums, parks, roads, bridges, and subways to prepare for the Olympics.

Finally, opening day arrived. August 8, 2008, was an auspicious date in China, where eight is considered a lucky number. A crowd of 91,000 people packed China's newly built National Stadium, nicknamed the "Bird's Nest." About two billion more viewers assembled in front of television sets around the world. That's one third of the world's population. At precisely 8 P.M. Beijing time, the opening ceremonies began.

A NIGHT TO REMEMBER

The Beijing ceremonies were the largest and most expensive in Olympic history. Directed by China's most famous filmmaker, Zhang Yimou, the production was a celebration of traditional Chinese history and culture. It also focused on the theme of harmony among nations.

The spectacular performance featured 2,008 drummers. Two hours' worth of music was composed just for the event. Fifteen thousand performers

55

wore costumes designed in 47 different styles. Acrobats floated down from the ceiling on guide wires, and brilliant fireworks burst in the night sky above the stadium. The final bill for the evening was reportedly tens of millions of dollars.

Most observers said they were dazzled. Reviewers pronounced the evening a rousing success. One journalist called the ceremonies "astonishing," while another reporter said the Bird's Nest was "alive with excitement."

WORLDWIDE PROTESTS

But the ceremonies were not without controversy. In the weeks leading up to 8/8/2008, crowds gathered in cities around the world to protest China's human rights record and its continued occupation of Tibet.

Protesters urged world leaders to boycott the ceremonies. German chancellor Angela Merkel and Prince Charles of Great Britain did, in fact, stay home. U.S. President George W. Bush attended the ceremonies but urged Chinese President Hu Jintao to engage in talks with the Dalai Lama's representatives.

Still, most Chinese people felt immense pride in the success of the ceremonies. "For a lot of foreigners, the only image of China comes from old movies that make us look poor and pathetic," said one Beijing resident. "Now look at us. We showed the world we can build new subways and beautiful modern buildings. The Olympics will redefine the way people see us."

GRAND FINALE: The opening ceremonies ended with fireworks exploding above the Bird's Nest stadium.

WINNERS: China's gymnasts celebrate winning gold in the team event.

WINNING GOLD

China wins the most gold medals.

More than 10,000 athletes from 204 countries competed in the 2008 Olympics in Beijing. With a total of 110 medals, the overall winner was the U.S. But China collected more gold than any other country. Its athletes won a grand total of 51 gold medals.

But China did much more than win gold. The host country impressed the world with its friendliness and efficiency, and the well-run Olympics were widely praised. What's more, China showed the world that it's an innovative and modern nation. Its influence extends far beyond the world of business—it has become a leading force in science, technology, and the arts.

As Nicholas D. Kristof of the *New York Times* put it: "The most important thing going on in the world today is the rise of China—in the Olympics and in almost every other facet of life."

ALL SMILES: Zou Shiming won a gold medal in boxing.

TIMELINE

Here's a look at some major events in China's recent history.

1949: With popular support from millions of peasants, Mao Zedong establishes the People's Republic of China as a communist nation.

1950: China seizes Tibet.

1958: Mao announces a plan to modernize the economy called the Great Leap Forward. The long-term consequences are disastrous.

1966: Mao launches the Cultural Revolution in order to silence his critics. He mobilizes millions of young supporters—called Red Guards—to back him.

1972: Richard Nixon is the first U.S. president to visit China.

1976: Mao dies.

1978: Deng Xiaoping, China's new leader, opens the country to foreign investment and encourages citizens to start businesses. These changes lead to an economic boom that continues today.

1979: The one-child policy is introduced as a way to control population growth.

1989: The Chinese government cracks down on student-led, pro-democracy protests in Beijing's Tiananmen Square.

1990: The Shanghai Stock Exchange opens.

1992: The first McDonald's opens in Beijing.

2003: China becomes the third country to send a person into space.

2004: Wal-Mart reports that 70 percent of its products are made in China.

2005: China's 1.3 billionth citizen is born.

2006: Construction of the main wall of the Three Gorges Dam, the world's biggest dam, is completed.

2008: China hosts the Olympics and shows itself off as a modern economic superpower.

2009: A new U.S. president takes over. With the world's economy in turmoil, economic relations with China are a top agenda item.

Resources

Looking for more information? Here are some resources you don't want to miss.

WEBSITES

World Factbook: China
https://www.cia.gov/library/publications/the-world-factbook/geos/ch.html

For a brief overview of China, check out this profile from the CIA.

China.org.cn

This multi-language site, authorized by the Chinese government, reports the latest news from China.

The Library of Congress
A Country Study: China
http://lcweb2.loc.gov/frd/cs/cntoc.html

A comprehensive study of China's history, geography, culture, economy, religion, and political climate.

China National Tourist Office
About China
http://www.cnto.org/aboutchina.asp

Geared toward tourists, this site covers China from A to Z, including attractions in many of China's cities.

Frontline
The Tank Man: The Memory of Tiananmen 1989
http://www.pbs.org/wgbh/pages/frontline/tankman

Information about a TV program that focuses on a central event in China's recent history, the Tiananmen Square protests.

BOOKS

Gay, Kathlyn. *Mao Zedong's China* (Dictatorships). Minneapolis: Twenty-First Century Books, 2008.

Haugen, David M., ed. *China* (Opposing Viewpoints). Farmington Hills, MI: Greenhaven Press, 2006.

Ma Yan and Pierre Haski. *The Diary of Ma Yan: The Struggles and Hopes of a Chinese Schoolgirl*. New York: HarperCollins, 2005.

Streissguth, Tom. *China in the 21st Century: A New World Power* (Issues in Focus Today). Berkeley Heights, NJ: Enslow Publishers, 2008.

Dictionary

A

activist (AK-tih-vist) *noun* a person who works to bring about social change

B

ban (BAN) *verb* to disallow or to make illegal

Buddhism (BOO-dih-zuhm) *noun* a religion based on the spiritual teachings of Siddhartha Gautama, also known as the Buddha, who lived in ancient India

C

capitalist (KA-pih-tuh-liz-uhm) *adjective* describes an economic system in which the people, not the government, own businesses and compete to sell their goods

censor (SEN-sir) *noun* a person who deletes or changes objectionable parts of literature, films, news reports, and other sources of information

communism (KAHM-yuh-ni-zuhm) *noun* an economic system in which the government owns a nation's resources and controls its economy

condemning (kuhn-DEM-ing) *verb* declaring something as wrong or evil

corrupt (kuh-RUPT) *adjective* seeking private gain at the expense of the public good

crackdown (KRAK-down) *noun* using force to stop a protest or movement

D

demonstration (deh-muhn-STRAY-shun) *noun* a public display of feelings about a cause, person, or event

dissidents (DIH-suh-dentz) *noun* people who actively oppose the government in power

F

firewall (FYE-uhr-wahl) *noun* technology that blocks access to certain information on the Internet

free market (free MAR-kit) *noun* an economic system in which prices and wages are not determined by the government and businesses compete freely against each other

G

greenhouse gases (GREEN-haus GAS-uhz) *noun* any gas that traps heat in Earth's atmosphere

H

human rights (HYOO-muhn RYTES) *noun* basic rights such as the freedoms of speech and religion, and the right to a fair trial

I

interrogation (in-TEH-ruh-GAY-shun) *noun* intense, in-depth questioning of a suspect

M

modernize (MAH-der-nyze) *verb* to adopt up-to-date ways of living

P

political prisoner (puh-LIH-tih-kuhl PRIZ-uh-ner) *noun* someone who is jailed because the government views him or her as a threat to its power

protest (PRO-test) *noun* an organized public expression of disapproval

S

solitary confinement (SAW-luh-tayr-ee kuhn-FYNE-ment) *noun* imprisonment by oneself, often in a dark room

superpower (SOO-per-PAU-wuhr) *noun* a country that plays a dominant political, economic, and military role in global affairs

surveillance (ser-VAY-luhntz) *noun* close watch over something or someone

T

toxins (TAHKS-inz) *noun* poisonous substances

Index

Photo Credits: Photographs © 2009: Alamy Images: 7 bottom left (blickwinkel/Wothe), 7 center right (Derek Brown/dbimages); Courtesy of Anna DeSanctis: 43; AP Images: 29, 32 (Greg Baker), 48 (Oded Balilty), 5 center, 26, 27 (Mike Fiala), 24 (ho), 6 top, 54 (Itsuo Inouye), 55 (Thomas Kienzle), 21 bottom (Stephan Savoia), 20 (Jeff Widener), 4 left (Chen Xie/Xinhua), 25 top (Liu Yu/Xinhua), 5 top, 10, 11; Contact Press Images: 22 (Greg Girard), 17 (Kenneth Jarecke); Corbis Images: 12, 16 top (Bettmann), 6 center top (Dennis Degnan), 5 bottom, 38, 39 (Xiaoyang Liu), 53 top (Ryan Pyle), 23 (Joseph Sohm/Visions of America), 7 top, 18, 19 (Peter Turnley), 21 top (David Turnley); Craig Simons: 40, 41 top; Getty Images: 57 top (Al Bello), back cover (Tom Bonaventure), 51 (Frederic J. Brown/AFP), 35 (Matt Campbell/AFP), 3 (Jerry Driendl), 16 bottom (Yann Layma), 30 (Feng Li); ImagineChina/Jiang Ren: 37; Courtesy of Jennifer 8. Lee: 41 bottom; Landov, LLC: 50 (Claro Cortes IV/Reuters), 56, 57 bottom (Chen Kai/Xinhua), 34 (Andrew Wong/Reuters), 7 center left (Yang Zi/Xinhua); Leif Parsons: 52; Lonely Planet Images/Greg Elms: 4 top right, 6 bottom left; Magnum Photos: 33 (Stuart Franklin), 25 bottom (Steve McCurry), 14 (New China Pictures), 31 (Martin Parr), 15 (Marc Riboud); National Geographic Image Collection/Fritz Hoffmann: cover; NEWSCOM/Paul Hilton/EPA: 49; Panos Pictures/Qilai Shen: 36, 53 bottom; Courtesy of Pierre Haskii: 44; Redux Pictures/Alan Riding/The New York Times: 45; Sinopix Photo Agency Limited/Richard Jones: 2, 28; Steven Harris: 7 bottom right, 46; The Image Works: 6 bottom right (Fritz Hoffmann), 6 center bottom (Liu Weixiong/Panorama); Vector-Images.com: 4 bottom right, 8 left; www.Flickr.com/MakZhou: 1; Zuma Press: 42 (CNS/ImagineChina), 47 (Li Jianbin/ImagineChina). Map by David Lindroth, Inc.

About This Book

The articles in this book were adapted from pieces that appeared originally in Scholastic magazines. Sources include the following:

1976–1995: GOOD-BYE TO CHAIRMAN MAO

Junior Scholastic: Vol. 92, issue 1, September 8, 1989; Vol. 96, issue 8, December 3, 1993; Vol. 97, issue 12, February 10, 1995

Scholastic Update: Vol. 121, issue 17, May 5, 1989; Vol. 122, issue 1, September 8, 1989; Vol. 125, issue 2, September 18, 1992; Vol. 125, issue 2, September 18, 1992

New York Times Upfront: Vol. 139, issue 7, December 11, 2006

1996–1999: TO GET RICH IS GLORIOUS

Junior Scholastic: Vol. 98, issue 12, February 9, 1996; Vol. 101, issue 12, February 8, 1999; Vol. 103, issue 1, September 4, 2000

Scholastic Update: Vol. 128, issue 12, March 22, 1996; Vol. 130, issue 2, September 22, 1997

New York Times Upfront: Vol. 131, issue 14, May 10, 1999; Vol. 132, issue 2, September 20, 1999

THE 21ST CENTURY: THE CHINESE CENTURY?

Junior Scholastic: Vol. 105, issue 18, May 9, 2003; Vol. 107, issue 8, November 29, 2004; Vol. 108, issue 6, October 31, 2005

New York Times Upfront: Vol. 133, issue 12, February 19, 2001; Vol. 137, issue 8, January 10, 2005; Vol. 137, issue 12, March 28, 2005; Vol. 138, issue 8, January 9, 2006; Vol. 138, issue 12, April 3, 2006; Vol. 139, issue 1, September 4, 2006; Vol. 140, issue 4/5, October 22–November 5, 2007; Vol. 140, issue 11, March 10, 2008

Scholastic News 5/6: Vol. 76, issue 5, October 8, 2007

Scholastic Scope: Vol. 53, issue 12, February 7, 2005

CONTENT CONSULTANT: Mark C. Elliott, Department of East Asian Languages and Civilizations, Harvard University